Sue Lawrence is known throughout Britain and beyond as a food writer and journalist. In addition to regular appearances on TV since she won BBC's *Masterchef* in 1991, she has also written many books on cooking and baking, including *The Scottish Kitchen* (2007) *The Sue Lawrence Book of Baking* (2004), *Eating In* (2011), and most recently, *Scottish Baking* (2014).

The *Scottish Berries* Bible

Sue Lawrence

Illustrated by Bob Dewar

BIRLINN

In loving memory of my father,
Bob Anderson
1923–2014

First published in 2015 by
Birlinn Limited
West Newington House
10 Newington Road
Edinburgh
EH9 1QS

www.birlinn.co.uk

ISBN: 978 1 78027 266 5

British Library Cataloguing-in-Publication Data
A catalogue record for this book is available
from the British Library

Designed and typeset by Mark Blackadder

Printed and bound by Gutenberg Press Ltd, Malta

Contents

Scottish Berries   9

Blackcurrant

    Duck with warm blackcurrant vinaigrette   14
    Roast pheasant with skirlie   15
      and blackcurrants
    Blackcurrant crumble cake   17
    Blackcurrant pie   19
    Black cap pudding   22
    Blackcurrant and muesli muffins   24

Blaeberries (Blueberries)

    Roast grouse with blaeberries   28
    Blaeberry grunt   30
    Blaeberry friands   33
    Blaeberry polenta crunch cake   34
    Spiced blaeberry loaf   37
    Panettone French toast with   38
      warm blaeberries
    Gluten-free blaeberry muffins   40

Bramble (Blackberry)

Bramble cobbler 42
Bramble and lemon curd 44
Bramble clafoutis 47
Bramble yoghurt scones 48
Hot berry sandwich 49
Bramble and butterscotch crumble tart 50
Banana and bramble oaty muffins 52

Gooseberry

Duck with gooseberries 57
Mackerel with gooseberry sauce 58
Gooseberry fool 59
Gooseberry streusel cake 60
Gooseberry and sweet cicely cheesecake 62

Raspberry

Pigeon breasts with raspberries 67
Raspberry and Drambuie tart 68
Raspberry cranachan 71
Quick raspberry ice-cream 72
Raspberry jam 73
Scots trifle 75
Raspberries with white chocolate 77
    and pine nuts
Chocolate and raspberry brownies 79
Raspberry and pine-nut muffins 80

Mascarpone, honey and raspberry tart 82
Berry cheesecake with polenta crust 83

Redcurrant
Redcurrant parfait 86
Squishy meringue berry roll 87
Redcurrant apple lattice pie 89

Strawberry
Strawberry daiquiri 92
Strawberry risotto 93
Berries with rosewater cream 94
Chilled strawberry and mint soup 96
Strawberry, cream cheese and 97
    balsamic ice-cream
Strawberry, mango and champagne salad 99
Strawberry and marshmallow salad 100
Berry tarts with bay cream 101
Red fruit salad 103
Strawberries with lavender ice-cream 104
Whole strawberry jam 105

Tayberry
Tayberry coulis 108
Warm berry compote with 109
    rose-petal ice-cream
Tayberry and blackcurrant slump 111

Scottish Berries

My thoughts on tasting the first berry of the season are not of Melba sauce, clotted cream or jam, but of luggies, dreels and red-dyed fingernails. For I was one of that happy band of berry-pickers who were paid a paltry sum of money to pick berries all day long in sun, rain or wind, for the whole month of July. In Angus and Perthshire, summer holidays and berries were inextricably linked. Hordes of school-children would walk, cycle or catch a bus to 'go to the berries'. It was a way of life, and the irritating scratches and red-stained T-shirts were part and parcel of the experience.

On arrival at the fruit farm in the morning, we would collect our buckets (called luggies) and tie them onto our waists with string. Then we would be dispatched to the fields – mainly of raspberries, but if you were unlucky, you were off on the back of a tractor over bumpy terrain to blackcurrant bushes. Apart from their inky black stains, they were impossible to pick without squashing them into jam between eager fingers. Gooseberries were also unpopular as they were prickly and tasted sour; redcurrants were as bad as blackcurrants. No, best of all were raspberries, as your back didn't ache as it did with strawberries. You were sheltered from the worst vagaries of the weather by the high leafy canes. And because of the length of the rows (called dreels) you could have deep or meaningless conversations with your fellow pickers if the appeal of devouring more forbidden fruit began to pall.

The trouble with raspberries was that they tasted so good, most of the ones I picked never made it into my luggie. My smile must have been rather unsightly, with recalcitrant little seeds sticking between every tooth. Raspberry pips are, perhaps surprisingly, of great historic significance as they were found in glacial deposits in the Scottish Lowlands – proof that the wild berry has been with us for quite some time. Scotland has retained its claim to be the world's best raspberry grower because of its cool, moist climate. These days, raspberry canes are spine-free, so itinerant pickers need not worry about

THE VERY BERRY

scratches and cuts as we did. Besides, most of the industrial fruit-picking is now done by machine.

The tayberry (a cross between a raspberry and black-berry) was under development while I was picking in Invergowrie near Dundee, at what is now the Scottish Crop Research Institute.

Blaeberries are wild and often to be found near the summits of Scottish mountains, perfect reward for climbing 3,000 or so feet on a dreich Scottish summer day. Brambles are another wild berry, cultivated under the name black-berry, but it is the wild fruit that has the intensely sharp taste and simply sings of late summer and autumn.

Back at the fruit farm, at the end of a long berry-picking day there was a stream of weary children strug-gling with their luggies to the weighing area. Some managed to pick pound upon pound of berries in a day; I resented their proficiency. Others contrived to cheat by concealing stones or liquids in the bottom of their luggies; I rather envied their audacity. Others – myself included – just smiled that seedy smile and resolved that next day more berries would go into the luggie, not into the mouth.

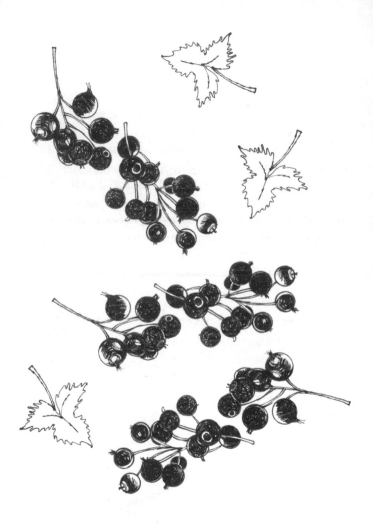

Blackcurrant

A popular garden bush in many Scottish gardens, blackcurrants are also cultivated on fruit farms. Versatile and used in both sweet and savoury recipes, blackcurrants can be frozen, but only if you are sieving when using in cooking as it's difficult to get rid of the stalks after they have been frozen.

Duck with warm blackcurrant vinaigrette

Serve with sauté potatoes and watercress salad.

Serves 6
6 duck breasts
300g blackcurrants
3 tbsps blackcurrant or raspberry vinegar
2 level tbsps light muscovado sugar
3 tbsps extra-virgin olive oil

Heat a frying pan until very hot.

Score the skin of each breast twice, then place in the hot pan, skin-side down, without added fat. You might need to do this in two batches. Season the flesh with salt and pepper. Cook for 2–3 minutes until brown, turn over and cook for a further 1 minute. Remove to a baking sheet and place in a preheated oven (220°C/425°F/Gas 7) for about 10 minutes (depending on thickness), then remove and allow to rest for 5–10 minutes. (The meat should be medium-rare; it will be medium after resting.)

For the vinaigrette, place the currants, vinegar and sugar in a pan and heat gently until the sugar dissolves. Increase the heat to medium and simmer for 2–3 minutes until the skins burst. Remove from the heat, then stir in the oil and salt and pepper to taste. Thickly slice the duck and serve with the vinaigrette.

Roast pheasant with skirlie and blackcurrants

The skirlie can be made in advance, then loosely covered in foil and reheated in a medium oven for about 10 minutes or until piping hot.

Serves 3–4
1 tbsp olive oil
25g butter
1 oven-ready pheasant (1.25–1.3kg)
100ml gin
200ml tub of crème fraiche
2 tbsps blackcurrant jelly
200g blackcurrants

For the skirlie
50g dripping (or 25g butter and 2 tbsps olive oil)
1 medium onion, peeled and very finely chopped
100g oatmeal (medium is most common; I like half medium
    and half pinhead for a nutty texture)

For the pheasant, heat the butter and oil in a roasting tin and brown the pheasant all over. Baste well with the fat, then season all over (which can take up to 5 minutes). Place in a preheated oven (200°C/400°F/Gas 6) for about 45 minutes or until done. Test by piercing the meat near the thigh and leg joint: the juices should be a very pale pink (not reddish pink). Baste 2–3 times as it roasts.

Remove the bird to a carving dish and keep warm, loosely covered with foil. Allow to rest for at least 10 minutes.

Heat the roasting tin on your gas or electric hob and add the gin. (Do this carefully if you are cooking over a naked flame.) Bubble away for 3–4 minutes, scraping up all the juices, then add the crème fraiche and jelly. Stirring well, cook gently for 4–5 minutes until slightly thickened. Add the currants and salt and pepper to taste, heating for a further couple of minutes until it is all piping hot. Check the seasoning again.

To serve, carve the pheasant, then serve with some sauce and a mound of skirlie.

To make the skirlie, heat the fat in a frying pan, add the onion and cook slowly for about 10 minutes until softened. Add the oatmeal, stirring until the fat is absorbed. Cook over a medium heat for about 10 minutes or until toasted and crumbly. Season to taste.

Blackcurrant crumble cake

This can be served warm for pudding with cream or yoghurt, or cold with your afternoon cup of tea. Raspberries are also good in this recipe, but if using them decrease the sugar in the crumble topping by about 40g.

Makes 24 squares
For the base
350g plain flour, sifted
50g caster sugar
200g unsalted butter, diced
2 medium free-range eggs, beaten

For the filling and crumble
75g plain flour, sifted
75g porridge oats
150g caster sugar
125g unsalted butter, diced
1 rounded tsp ground cinnamon
zest of 1 unwaxed lemon
2 level tbsps semolina
500g blackcurrants

Preheat the oven to 200°C/400°F/Gas 6. Butter a Swiss roll tin (23 x 33cm/9 x 13in)

For the base, place the flour, sugar and butter in a food processor with a pinch of salt and process briefly until it resembles breadcrumbs. Slowly add the eggs through the feeder tube and process very briefly, until just combined. Press the dough into your prepared tin, levelling it out.

For the crumble, place the flour, oats, sugar, butter, cinnamon and lemon zest in a bowl, then rub in the butter until crumbly.

Scatter the semolina over the base in the tin, then tip in the blackcurrants, distributing them as evenly as possible. Top with the crumble and very gently press down, trying to cover most of the currants.

Bake for 20 minutes, then turn down the oven to 180°C/350°F/Gas 4 and continue to bake for about 30 minutes further, or until golden brown.

Leave to cool for about 30 minutes, then cut into squares and remove to a wire rack.

Blackcurrants

Blackcurrant pie

This is a free-form pie, made on a baking tray rather than within the confines of a tart tin. It resembles those I used to love in northern Finland, where the berries used were bilberries or lingonberries.

Serves 6
For the pastry
225g plain flour
25g icing sugar
150g butter, diced
1 large free-range egg, beaten
1 egg-white
caster sugar, to sprinkle

For the filling
500g blackcurrants
75g caster sugar
1 tbsp semolina

For the pastry, sift the flour into a food processor and add the sugar and diced butter. Process briefly till it resembles breadcrumbs, then add the whole egg and process until moist. (Add a splash of water if necessary.) Bring together to a ball. Unroll a large wide sheet of clingfilm, put the dough in the middle and then place another sheet of clingfilm on top. Roll out the pastry – through the film –

Pastry

Filling

semolina

with a rolling pin till you have a circle approximately
30–32cm in diameter. Remove to the fridge for an hour
or so.

For the filling, combine the currants with the sugar
and semolina.

Peel away one sheet of clingfilm, place the pastry on
buttered baking sheet and then peel off the top layer of
film. Put the fruit mixture in the middle, then spread out
to about 4cm from the edge. Fold in the dough a little to
form the crust. Brush all round the crust with egg-white
and sprinkle with caster sugar.

Bake at 200°C/400°F/Gas 6 for about 30–35
minutes until the crust is golden. Serve with thick
yoghurt or whipped cream.

Black cap pudding

Black cap pudding was originally a boiled batter pudding with a cap of buttery dried currants and mixed peel. My version is a light steamed pudding with a sticky summit of blackcurrant jam, which I prefer for its rich gloss and fruity tang. Serve with oodles of custard.

Serves 6
2 heaped tbsps blackcurrant jam
110g unsalted butter, softened
110g caster sugar
2 large free-range eggs
175g self-raising flour, sifted
grated zest of 1 lemon
2 tbsps milk

Butter a 1-litre pudding basin and put the jam in the bottom. Cream together the butter and sugar until light and fluffy, then beat in the eggs, one at a time, adding a little of the flour with each egg.

Using a metal spoon, fold in the remaining flour, a pinch of salt, the lemon and the milk. Once thoroughly combined, spoon the mixture carefully on top of the jam. Smooth over the top.

To cover, fold a pleat in a doubled, buttered piece of foil (to allow room for expansion) and tie it securely over the top with string. (I always make a string handle by threading the string twice from one side to the other, so

the pudding is easy to lift.) Scrunch up the foil at the sides, so it does not hang down into the water.

Place the basin in a large saucepan over a low heat, then pour boiling water carefully down the side to come about halfway up the basin – the water should simmer gently, rather than be boiling furiously. Cover the saucepan with a tight lid. Steam for 1¾–2 hours, topping up the water level if necessary, then remove the basin carefully.

Wait for about 10 minutes, then remove the foil and run a knife around the edges of the basin. Now place a serving plate on top and carefully invert, so the pudding ends up upright on the plate, with the blackcurrant jam glistening seductively on top.

Blackcurrant and muesli muffins

Don't use muesli with too many big nuts or large chunks
of fruit.

Makes 15

100g dried apricots, chopped
grated zest and juice of 1 orange
150ml soured cream
100g butter, melted
3 tbsps runny honey
2 free-range eggs
175g self-raising flour
125g wholemeal self-raising flour
1 level tsp baking powder
75g muesli
blackcurrant jam

For the topping
50g light muscovado sugar
½ tsp ground cinnamon
1 heaped tbsp plain flour
30g butter, melted
50g toasted muesli

Soak the apricots in the juice for about 20 minutes, then
combine the cream, butter, honey and eggs together. Stir
in the apricot mixture.

In a separate bowl, sift the flours and the baking
powder, add the muesli and stir in the apricot mixture.

Spoon into paper cases in a muffin tray, make a thumbprint in the middle of each and add a heaped teaspoon of jam.

Combine the topping ingredients and sprinkle over the jam, pressing down gently to cover. Bake at 190°C/375°F/Gas 5 for about 20 minutes or until well risen.

Blaeberries (Blueberries)

Also known as bilberries, blaeberries grow wild
on Scottish hills. Since they are very tiny, they are
seldom cultivated, but blueberries, which are
slightly larger, are often found on fruit farms.
Blueberries can be used in all these recipes instead
of blaeberries. They freeze well.

Roast grouse with blaeberries

The beginning of the grouse season is not a good time to cook grouse. For a start, there is so much hype, with chefs having the poor birds flown in straight from the moor in time for dinner on the 12th, without them being hung at all; and also they are ridiculously expensive. Better to wait until early September, then enjoy the young grouse for the entire month until the older birds come in for casseroling. This simple roast dish calls for grouse to be stuffed with a mixture of butter and blaeberries, covered with bacon to prevent drying out, then to be roasted in a very hot oven and well rested to cook evenly.

Serves 2

2 young grouse, oven-ready
125g blaeberries (or blueberries)
50g butter, softened
6 rashers unsmoked back bacon
1 tbsp bramble jelly
2 tbsps red wine

Wash out the insides of the grouse and dry well. Mix the berries into the butter (gently, so they do not burst) and season with salt and pepper. Stuff this mixture into each body cavity. Cover with the bacon, trying to cover all the breast. Place in a buttered roasting tin and roast at 230°C/450°F/Gas 8 for 20 minutes, then remove from the oven. Tip out the contents of the birds' cavities back into the tin. Place the birds on a serving dish to rest in a low oven (if you have only one oven, leave in the oven with the door open) for at least 10 minutes, loosely covered with foil. Place the tin over a direct heat, add the jelly and wine and bubble away for 2–3 minutes and then season to taste. Pour the contents into a small sauce boat and serve with the grouse.

Blaeberry grunt

I first came across a grunt in a very old Canadian cookbook from a time when all puddings were boiled and the noise of the pudding phut-phutting in the simmering water for hours on end was like a reassuring grunt! Nowadays most puddings are baked in the oven, but the name remains. It is not dissimilar to a crumble or cobbler in concept. Serve warm with thick cream.

Serves 6
600g blaeberries (or blueberries)
100g caster sugar
2 level tsps cornflour
3 tbsps lemon juice
175g self-raising flour
1 level tsp baking powder
zest of 1 lemon
50g butter, diced
1 medium free-range egg, beaten
4 tbsps milk

Place the berries in a saucepan with 50g of sugar. Dissolve the cornflour in the lemon juice and add to the pan. Bring very slowly to the boil. Boil for about 2 minutes, until the juices are released, then remove from the heat and tip everything into a shallow oven dish. Sift the flour and baking powder into a bowl and stir in the remaining 50g of sugar and lemon zest. Rub in the

butter, then stir in the egg and milk to form a soft dough.
Drop 6 spoonfuls of the dough over the top of the
berries – they do not need to be too shapely as they will
spread out haphazardly during cooking. Bake in a
preheated oven (220°C/425°F/Gas 7) for about 20
minutes until the topping is golden brown and firm.
Serve warm with thick cream.

4 EGG WHITES

BUTTER

GROUND ALMONDS

Moulds

PLAIN FLOUR

ICING SUGAR

Blaeberry friands

I was introduced to friands in Australia in the 1990s
where they were hugely popular – and still are today.
Make these in shallow bun tins or mini muffin tins, or,
best of all, small oval-shaped moulds.

Makes about 20
50g plain flour
200g icing sugar
100g ground almonds
140g unsalted butter, melted
4 large free-range egg-whites
125g blaeberries (or blueberries)

Sift the flour and icing sugar into a bowl and stir in the
almonds.

Combine the melted butter with the flour mixture.

Whisk the egg-whites with a pinch of salt until there
are soft peaks (not stiff ones) and fold in a spoonful of the
egg-whites into the mixture. Gradually and gently fold in
the rest, then fold in the berries carefully, so they do not
bruise.

Spoon into well-buttered little moulds and bake at
200°C/400°F/Gas 6 for 15–20 minutes or until puffed
up and golden brown. Remove from the moulds after a
minute or so to a wire rack to cool completely.

Blaeberry polenta crunch cake

This cake has a nice crunch to it and is ideal for pudding or afternoon tea.

Serves 8

100g polenta and 2 tsps polenta
250g self-raising flour, sifted
150g golden caster sugar
grated zest of 1 lemon
150g unsalted butter, diced
1 large free-range egg
1 tbsp freshly squeezed lemon juice
200g blaeberries (or blueberries)
25g natural demerara sugar

Place the polenta, flour and sugar in a food processor with a pinch of salt and process for a few seconds, then add the butter and process again until it resembles bread-crumbs.

Add the egg and lemon juice and process very briefly until just combined.

Tip about two-thirds of this mixture into a buttered 24cm loose-bottomed springform cake tin, pressing down all over.

Sprinkle 2 teaspoons of polenta over this base, then scatter over the berries. Sprinkle the demerara sugar over the top, crumbling the remaining polenta mixture over to more or less cover. Press down very lightly and bake in a preheated oven (180°C/350°F/Gas 4) for about 35 minutes or until golden brown. Cool on a wire rack for 20 minutes or so then remove the sides. Serve warm or cold with thick yoghurt or crème fraiche.

Spiced blaeberry loaf

You can use ricotta instead of cottage cheese if you prefer.

Serves 10
225g self-raising flour
½ tsp cinnamon
½ tsp ground ginger
55g semolina
110g caster sugar
grated zest of 1 small orange
1 large free-range egg
55g cottage cheese
110ml sunflower oil
1 tbsp orange juice
200g blaeberries (or blueberries)

Sift the flour and spices into a bowl and stir in the semolina, sugar and orange zest.

Whisk together the egg, cheese, oil and juice and stir into the dry ingredients.

Spoon two-thirds of the mixture into a buttered 900g loaf tin. Press down, and top with the berries. Sprinkle over the remaining mixture as if for a crumble, then pat down gently with your hand.

Bake in a preheated oven (180°C/350°F/Gas 4) for about 40 minutes or until golden-brown and cooked through. Cool on a wire rack and then turn out.

Panettone French toast with warm blaeberries

This is ideal to make with left-over Christmas panettone.

Serves 4
panettone
2 medium free-range eggs
300ml full-fat milk
25g golden caster sugar and extra to sprinkle
75g butter
25g golden icing sugar
225g blaeberries (or blueberries)
zest of 1 lemon

Cut two thick rounds from your panettone: about 1.5–2 cm thick. Cut these into quarters.

Whisk together the eggs, milk and caster sugar. Pour into a wide deep bowl and add the eight panettone quarters. Soak for 4–5 minutes, turning once or twice, until the custard is completely absorbed.

Heat 30g butter in a large frying pan and, once it is bubbling, add four of the panettone quarters. Over a medium heat, fry for 2–3 minutes on each side, until golden brown. Transfer onto paper towel to drain and keep warm. Add another 30g butter to the pan and fry the remaining four quarters.

Meanwhile, melt the remaining 25g butter and the

icing sugar in a small frying pan over a low heat. Once melted, increase the heat to medium, add the berries and cook for 2–3 minutes, stirring occasionally, then remove from the heat and stir in the lemon zest.

Sprinkle the French toast with caster sugar and serve with some berries.

Gluten-free blaeberry muffins

I think these are even more delicious than a regular
blueberry muffin – a little crunchy from the ground rice,
they are moist and delicious!

Makes 12
150g rice flour (ground rice)
100g ground almonds
1½ tsps baking powder
½ tsp bicarbonate of soda
50g desiccated coconut
75g light muscovado sugar
grated zest of 1 orange
75ml sunflower oil
100ml milk
2 free-range eggs
150g blueberries (or blueberries)

Combine the first seven ingredients in a bowl.

Mix the oil, milk and eggs in a jug and pour into the
bowl, stirring slowly. Fold in the berries gently, then fill
12 muffin cases in a bun tray. Bake in a preheated oven
(190°C/375°F Gas 5) for 20 minutes or until risen and
golden.

Bramble (Blackberry)

Known as bramble in Scotland, the blackberry is
found wild in hedgerows, but is also increasingly
grown in fruit farms. If you are picking them in
the wild, watch out for the thorns! They are some
of the last berries to ripen in the season, and
freeze well.

Bramble cobbler

Serve warm with Greek yoghurt.

Serves 6
750g brambles
125g caster sugar
25g cornflour dissolved in 2 tbsps cold water
100g self-raising flour
75g fine polenta
1 tsp baking powder
½ tsp cinnamon
grated zest and juice of 1 lemon
50g butter, melted, cooled very slightly
75ml milk

Place the brambles, 75g of the sugar and 2 tablespoons of water in a pan and slowly heat until the sugar dissolves, stirring until it does so. Then increase the heat and add the cornflour mixture. Stir over a medium heat for 3 minutes until thickened. Stir in the brambles and tip into a round oven-proof dish, then cool.

For the cobbler topping, sieve the flour, polenta, baking powder, cinnamon and a pinch of salt into a bowl and add the remaining 50g of sugar and the lemon zest. Stir in the lemon juice and melted butter, then quickly stir in the milk. (Do not overwork the dough.)

Drop 6 spoonfuls of the cobbler mixture over the berries and bake at 200°C/400°F/Gas 6 for about 40 minutes or until the fruit bubbles up and the cobbles are cooked through. (Check by gently easing the top of one off with the point of a sharp knife and looking underneath.) Serve warm.

Bramble and lemon curd

Although I use the microwave method for curd, you can make it in the normal way in a bowl over a pan of simmering water, stirring all the time until thick.

To sterilise jars, wash them in hot soapy water, rinse and then dry in a low oven. Or put them through a dishwasher cycle, then microwave on High for 1½ minutes.

Makes 2 jars
150g brambles
100g unsalted butter, diced
200g granulated sugar
grated zest of 3 unwaxed lemons
175ml freshly squeezed lemon juice
3 large free-range eggs, beaten

Purée the berries in a food processor and set aside.

Place the butter, sugar, lemon zest and juice in a microwaveable bowl and cook, uncovered, on High, for 4–5 minutes, stirring once, until the butter is melted and the sugar dissolved. Remove and cool for a couple of minutes.

Place a plastic sieve over the bowl and push the eggs and blackberry purée through it, so that any blobby bits of the white and all bramble pips remain in the sieve.

Stir the mixture well, return to the microwave and

Brambles

cook for 5–6 minutes, removing from the microwave every 1 minute and whisking madly (otherwise it will scramble) – ensuring you get into all corners – until it thickens: it should have the consistency of lightly whipped cream. (It will firm up on cooling.) Spoon into two 350g warm, sterilised jars. Cover when completely cold and refrigerate for up to four weeks.

Bramble clafoutis

Classically made in southern France from cherries (or prunes steeped in Armagnac), this delectable sweet light batter pudding is even better with Scottish brambles. Though it emerges billowy and hot from the oven, it is best served either just warm with some pouring cream and perhaps a sploosh of bramble liqueur or kirsch – or wrap the dish once cold, and take on a picnic.

Serves 6

20g butter
250g brambles
50g plain flour
25g ground almonds
2 large free-range eggs
250ml full fat milk
50g caster sugar
2 tsps Demerara sugar, to sprinkle

Butter a 22cm oven dish generously with butter and put the brambles into it, in one layer. Place all other ingredients (except the Demerara sugar) in a food processor and whizz together until smooth (or whisk by hand with balloon whisk). Pour over the brambles and place in a preheated oven (190°C/375°F/Gas 5) for 30–35 minutes until puffed up and golden. Sprinkle with Demerara sugar and serve warm or cold.

Bramble yoghurt scones

The yoghurt in the scones produces, rather like the buttermilk and sour milk of old, a light, airy texture.

Makes 10–12

225g plain flour
2 heaped tsps baking powder
25g caster sugar
75g butter, cubed
3–4 tbsps natural yoghurt
100g brambles
milk

Sift the flour, baking powder and a pinch of salt into a bowl and stir in the sugar.

Rub in the butter, then add the yoghurt a little at a time. Add the brambles and bring the mixture together gently to a round. Add a splash of milk if necessary to achieve a stiff yet soft dough. Flatten the dough lightly with your hand and cut with a cutter into 10–12 rounds. Set on a buttered baking tray and brush the tops with milk.

Bake at 220°C/425°F/Gas 7 for 12–15 minutes until risen and golden. Transfer to a wire rack and cool, then serve with butter.

Hot berry sandwich

Use any combination of berries apart from strawberries, as they will become too soft.

Serves 4
600g brambles and raspberries
25g butter
25g golden caster sugar
4–5 tbsps gin
4 thick slices of Selkirk Bannock (or panettone),
    foil-wrapped and warmed in a low oven

Place the berries in a pan with the butter, sugar and gin. Heat slowly until the berries are warm and glazed; this will take 5–10 minutes.

Place the slices of bannock on four pudding dishes. Spoon the berries and liquid over and serve at once, with plenty of thick cream or yoghurt.

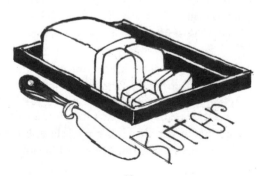

Bramble and butterscotch crumble tart

This is a lovely tart that can be served warm with thick or clotted cream – or with good vanilla ice-cream.

Serves 6
For the pastry
50g golden caster sugar
75g ground almonds
150g plain flour, sifted
110g butter, diced
1 large free-range egg

For the filling
1 heaped tbsp semolina
750g brambles
250g dulce de leche or tinned caramel

For the crumble
75g plain flour, sifted
50g medium oatmeal
75g golden granulated sugar
75g butter, diced

Make the pastry in the usual way, either by hand or in a food processor, by processing the first four ingredients together and then adding the egg. Once it is amalgamated, combine in your hands, wrap in clingfilm and chill well. (The pastry is softish.) Now roll it out to fit a

deep 23cm loose-bottomed, buttered flan tin. Prick the base and chill again for at least three hours, preferably overnight.

Sprinkle the semolina over the pastry and scatter the brambles on top. Warm the dulce de leche or caramel and spoon over the berries.

Make the crumble topping by mixing the flour, oatmeal and sugar and rubbing in the butter. Sprinkle over the berries and press down very lightly. Bake at 200°C/400°F/Gas 6 for 15 minutes, then reduce to 180°C/350°F/Gas 4 for 25–30 minutes or until golden brown. Leave until barely warm before carefully decanting to a plate.

Banana and bramble oaty muffins

These banana and bramble-flavoured crunchy oat-topped muffins are a doddle to prepare and take only 20 minutes to bake.

Makes 12 American-size muffins
150g butter, melted, cooled slightly
60g golden caster sugar
2 large free-range eggs, beaten
200ml milk
grated zest and juice of ½ a lemon
2 small ripe bananas, mashed
250g self-raising flour, sifted
250g brambles
40g jumbo (whole rolled) oats
40g light muscovado sugar

Place the first five ingredients in a bowl and stir to combine.

Stir in the bananas and then fold in the flour, with a gentle action. Now tip in the brambles and very lightly stir to combine: do not beat madly or the brambles will bleed purple into the mixture.

Spoon the mixture into 12 large muffin cases set in a bun tin. Combine the oats and the muscovado sugar and sprinkle some over the top of each.

Bake at 200°C/400°F/Gas 6 for about 20 minutes or until golden brown and cooked through. Eat warm.

GOOSEBERRIES

Gooseberry

The first of the soft fruits to ripen in Scotland, they were always known for their sharp tartness. But nowadays, eating varieties have been introduced and these are sweeter and so delicious to eat raw. Gooseberries can be frozen but top and tail them before freezing.

Duck with gooseberries

Serve with new potatoes and peas or green beans.

Serves 4
4 large duck breasts
1 tsp runny honey
400g gooseberries
40g caster sugar
150ml dry white wine
2–3 shallots, peeled and chopped
150ml chicken stock
2–3 large sage leaves

Heat a heavy frying pan to hot and add the duck, skin-side down. Brown, turning once, then remove to a roasting tray, skin-side up. (Keep the pan and the fat rendered in it.) Brush with honey and roast at 220°C/425°F/Gas 7 for 12–15 minutes, then allow to rest.

Meanwhile make the sauce: place the gooseberries in the pan with the sugar and wine, simmer till soft and then push through a coarse sieve.

In the pan the duck was fried in, heat the fat, add the shallots, fry gently for a few minutes, then add the stock and sage and bring to the boil. Reduce this to half, then add the gooseberry puree and simmer for a few minutes until it has a sauce-like consistency. Season to taste and serve on warm plates with the sliced duck on top.

Mackerel with gooseberry sauce

Herring is also good with gooseberry sauce.

Serves 4
8 small mackerel fillets, skin slashed
150g gooseberries, topped and tailed
fish stock
natural yoghurt
fennel fronds, optional

Grill the mackerel under a hot grill (without added fat) until just done – about 4–5 minutes on each side.

Meanwhile, cook the gooseberries in about 4 tablespoons of fish stock until tender, then puree, adding a little more stock if necessary. Add about 2 tablespoons of yoghurt and seasoning to taste.

Stir in a few chopped fennel fronds if using, and serve the fish with the sauce on the side.

Gooseberry fool

Serve with thin shortbread biscuits.

Serves 4
500g gooseberries, topped and tailed
50g caster sugar
400ml thick custard
150ml double cream, whisked to soft peaks

For the puree, place the berries in a pan with the sugar
and 1 tablespoon of water. Cook over a low heat for a
few minutes until just tender, cover and leave for 10
minutes or so before pureeing or mashing until smooth.

Then fold the custard into the cream and stir the
gooseberry puree gently in. Serve in pretty glasses.

Gooseberry streusel cake

I spent three years in the early 1990s living in northern Germany, where I ate many streusel cakes. Made often from cherries and sharp fruit and berries, they reminded me of homely Scottish crumble, and so I used to bake them often myself. Eat barely warm, or cold with whipped cream.

Serves 8

300g gooseberries
150g caster sugar
2 tbsps sweet white wine (e.g. Sauternes or Muscat)
175g plain flour, sifted
50g ground almonds
1 tsp baking powder
125g butter, diced
1 large free-range egg, beaten

Cook the gooseberries with 25g of the sugar and the wine, till soft. Drain well, reserving the liquid. Boil the liquid in a pan till reduced to half, then pour over the fruit. Cool.

Place the flour, almonds, the remaining 125g of sugar and baking powder in a food processor, blitz, then add butter and process until it resembles breadcrumbs. With the machine running, add the egg.

Press half of this mixture into a buttered, lined 20cm cake tin, then, using a slotted spoon, spread the

gooseberries over the base. Sprinkle the remaining
mixture over the gooseberries, as if adding the crumble
for a crumble topping. Bake at 180°C/350°F/Gas 4 for
50–60 minutes, testing with a wooden cocktail stick: no
wet mixture should adhere when it is cooked through.
Remove to a wire rack to cool.

Gooseberry and sweet cicely cheesecake

If you cannot find sweet cicely – a wonderful old-fashioned sweet aniseed herb – add a sploosh of elderflower cordial instead.

Serves 8

For the base
175g gingernuts, crushed
175g digestives, crushed
125g butter, melted

For the filling
400g cream cheese
2 free-range eggs
juice of 1 lemon
150g caster sugar
375g gooseberries, topped and tailed
1 heaped tbsp of sweet cicely, chopped

For the topping
300ml sour cream
50g caster sugar

Mix the biscuits and butter and press into the base of a deep 24cm loose-based cake tin. Chill.

For the filling, beat the cream cheese, eggs, lemon and 75g of the sugar together till smooth, then pour onto the base. Bake in a preheated oven (180°C/350°F/Gas 4)

for 30 minutes, remove and cool for 5–10 minutes.

Meanwhile, cook the gooseberries and the remaining 75g of sugar for about 10 minutes till soft, then drain over a sieve. Mash with the sweet cicely, using a potato masher. Spread over the cooled base.

Beat the topping ingredients together and slowly pour over the gooseberries. Bake for a further 15–20 minutes till just set. Turn off the heat and keep the cheesecake in the switched-off oven for an hour or so, to prevent cracks.

Serve at room temperature.

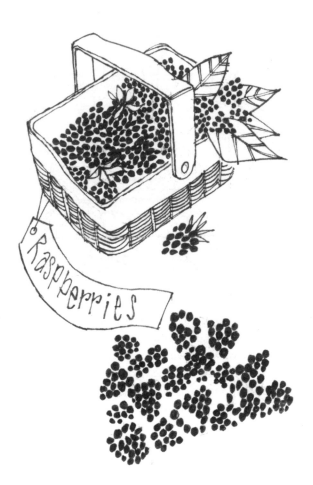

Raspberries

Raspberry

This is Scotland's best loved berry: every Scottish child is brought up with raspberries, if not picking them in the garden then eating them in jam on toast or for pudding with ice-cream. Related to the bramble, the raspberry has grown wild in Scotland for centuries, but now is found in gardens or on fruit farms. Raspberries freeze well.

Pappardelle

Raspberry VINEGAR

OLIVE OIL

PIGEON BREASTS [EIGHT]

CREME FRAICHE

Raspberries

Pigeon breasts with raspberries

Serve with pappardelle.

Serves 4
8 pigeon breasts
3 tbsps olive oil
2 tbsps raspberry vinegar
200g crème fraiche
150g raspberries
pappardelle, to serve

Place the pigeon breasts in a shallow bowl and pour over the oil. Using your hands, turn them in the oil, cover and leave for a couple of hours somewhere cool.

Heat a good, heavy frying pan to very hot (without any fat), and add the breasts and their oil. Brown on each side (about 2 minutes altogether) then remove to a baking sheet and place in a preheated oven (230°C/450°F/Gas 8) for 7–8 minutes or until still very pink. Allow to rest for 2–3 minutes, by which time the meat will transform from rare to medium.

In the frying pan, add the vinegar, stir around over high heat and add the crème fraiche, stirring as it reduces. After a couple of minutes, add the berries and stir again, squishing down about half the raspberries but leaving the rest whole. Taste and season accordingly.

Serve two pigeon breasts each on a pile of pappardelle with the sauce over the top.

Raspberry and Drambuie tart

Be sure to remove from the oven when just set and no more. It will firm up on cooling.

Serves 6
For the pastry
50g caster sugar
125g ground almonds
125g plain flour, sifted
125g butter, diced
1 medium free-range egg

For the filling
3 tbsps golden caster sugar
2 large free-range eggs
200ml tub of crème fraiche
2 tbsps Drambuie
250g raspberries

To serve
4 heaped tbsps crème fraiche
2 tbsps Drambuie

For the pastry, place the sugar, almonds, flour and butter in a food processor and process until it resembles bread-crumbs. Add the medium egg, process, gather the pastry into a ball, clingwrap, chill for one hour. Roll out to fit a deep 23cm tart tin. Prick the base and chill for at least four hours.

Line with foil and baking beans and bake at 190°C/375°F/Gas 5 for 15 minutes, remove the foil and the beans and bake for a further 10 minutes. Remove from the oven and cool.

For the filling, beat together the sugar, eggs, crème fraiche and Drambuie. Pour into the pastry case. Arrange the berries in a single layer on top. Bake for 35 minutes or until just set. Cool.

Beat crème fraiche and Drambuie together and serve with the tart.

Raspberry cranachan

Traditionally this is made with crowdie (a crofters' soft, fresh cheese). You can either make with all cream or add in some thick yoghurt to reduce the richness.

A wee piece of shortbread on the side never goes amiss.

Serves 4

2–3 tbsps pinhead oatmeal OR porridge oats
300ml double cream
runny honey
whisky to taste
100g tub thick yoghurt
300g raspberries (or brambles)

Toast the oatmeal, either under the grill or in a dry frying pan, and cool.

Lightly whip the cream with a good dessertspoon or two of honey and a good splash of whisky until floppy, then gently fold in the yoghurt and finally most of the oatmeal.

Fold in half the berries, pile into four glasses and decorate with the remaining berries, a drizzle of honey and a scattering of oatmeal.

Quick raspberry ice-cream

Easiest ice-cream ever!

Serves 4
250g raspberries, frozen
200ml crème fraiche
150ml natural yoghurt
2 tbsps golden caster sugar

Place everything in a food processor and whizz until
smooth, then taste and add more sugar as necessary. Serve
at once.

Raspberry jam

Raspberry jam was the one jam my mother always had whatever month it was, because we had so many raspberries at the bottom of our garden. Her blackcurrant and apple jellies would often run out by early spring, but raspberry jam lasted all year. I vividly remember the sweet heady aromas of jam wafting out through the kitchen door, luring me into the house from playing in the garden in those long halcyon days of childhood summers.

Makes 3 x 500g jars
1kg raspberries
1kg preserving sugar (granulated will also do)
a knob of unsalted butter
Drambuie (optional)

Place the raspberries in a large deep saucepan or preserving pan and simmer very gently for about 20 minutes, until they release their own juices. Add the sugar and heat gently until the sugar is dissolved, stirring constantly.

Add the butter, bring to the boil, then boil rapidly for about 25 minutes or longer until a setting-point is reached. During this time, it will splatter – but don't be tempted to reduce the heat. I'm afraid you'll just have to wipe up afterwards! Setting-point is determined by placing a few drops on a cold saucer and allowing it to cool quickly. Push it with your finger, and if it wrinkles, it is ready.

If using Drambuie, add a couple of tablespoons now. Stir, then pot in warm sterilised jars. Cool and place the lids on firmly when cold. Label and store somewhere dark.

Scots trifle

There are so many variations on trifle, an entire book could be written on the subject. But I must say we have some rather fine offerings in Scotland, with our wonderful raspberries, brambles – and of course a good supply of whisky or Drambuie to drench the sponges. This recipe is pretty boozy, so reduce the Drambuie by half and substitute fruit juice if children are to be given a helping.

Serves 8

5–6 trifle sponges, halved
raspberry jam
150g packet of ratafias (Italian almond macaroons)
5–6 tbsps Drambuie
350g fresh raspberries and a few extra to decorate
300ml double cream, lightly whipped

For the custard

600ml of creamy milk (or half milk, half double cream)
25g sugar
4 large free-range egg-yolks

First, make the custard: heat the milk (and cream if using) in a heavy saucepan until just bubbling. Remove from the heat. Beat the sugar and yolks together and slowly pour into the milk, whisking all the time. Return to a gentle heat and cook slowly, stirring or whisking, until slightly thickened (5–8 minutes). Do not allow to boil. Cool, stirring to prevent a skin forming.

Spread the sponges with jam and place in the base of a pretty glass dish. Scatter over most of the ratafias, keeping some behind for decoration. Slowly sprinkle over enough Drambuie to just soak all the sponges and ratafias. Do not drown them. Top with the raspberries, then pour over the cooled custard. Cover and chill. Shortly before serving, spread with the whipped cream and decorate with ratafias and raspberries.

Raspberries with white chocolate and pine nuts

Rasps go so well with white chocolate, the tart berry cutting through the sickly white stuff. Delicious!

Serves 2
25g pine nuts
250g raspberries
40g quality white chocolate, chilled

Heat the nuts in a non-stick frying pan for 2–3 minutes till golden brown, shaking the pan often. Tip onto kitchen paper to cool.

Place the berries in a bowl, top with the cooled pine nuts and then coarsely shave or grate the chocolate over the top. Serve chilled with some pouring cream.

Chocolate and raspberry brownies

Squishy and delicious, these should be made only with fresh berries: frozen berries will make the mixture too moist.

Makes 16
350g good quality dark chocolate
225g butter
3 large free-range eggs
250g dark muscovado sugar
100g plain flour
1 tsp baking powder
150g fresh raspberries

Melt the chocolate and butter together and cool slightly. Whisk the eggs until thick, add the sugar and beat till glossy.

Mix into the melted chocolate and then fold in the flour and baking powder.

Pour half of the mixture into a buttered 23cm brownie tin, scatter over the berries and cover with the remaining mixture. Bake at 170°C/325°F/Gas 3 for 35–40 minutes or until only a little mixture adheres to an inserted skewer.

Remove to a wire rack and cool completely before cutting.

Raspberry and pine-nut muffins

Serve these freshly baked, slightly warm if possible. They can also be frozen – then defrost by placing in a medium oven, still frozen, for about 20 minutes. Do not microwave them or they become soggy.

Makes 12

225g self-raising flour
1 level tsp baking powder
½ tsp cinnamon
100g golden caster sugar
1 large free-range egg
75ml sunflower oil
150ml tub of soured cream
150g raspberries
50g pine-nuts

Sieve the first three ingredients into a bowl and stir in the sugar.

Whisk together the egg, oil and soured cream, and gently fold this into the dry ingredients. Very gently fold in the berries and pine-nuts and spoon into 12 muffin cases set in a muffin tin and bake at 200°C/400°F/Gas 6 for 20–25 minutes until golden.

arpone, honey
raspberry tart

Decorate with edible rose petals if you like.

Serves 6
150g plain flour
50g ground almonds
100g butter, diced
1 tbsp golden caster sugar
1 large free-range egg
500g mascarpone
runny honey
1 tbsp rosewater
300g raspberries

For the pastry, whizz the flour, almonds, butter and sugar together in a food processor, then slowly add the egg, to combine to a dough. Clingwrap and chill. Once chilled, roll out thinly to line a deep 23cm tart tin. Fork all over and chill well once more, preferably overnight.

Blind bake (lined with foil and baking beans) at 200°C/ 400°F/Gas 6 for 25 minutes, remove the foil and beans and reduce to 180°C/350°F/Gas 4 and bake until cooked through – a further 5–10 minutes. Remove and cool.

Shortly before serving, beat the mascarpone with enough honey to flavour (about 3 tablespoons, but each honey varies in strength) and the rosewater. Fill the pastry case with this and scatter over the raspberries.

Berry cheesecake with polenta crust

Use any combination of berries.

Serves 8–10
For the base
75g plain flour, sifted
50g polenta
50g golden caster sugar
100g chilled butter, diced
1 medium egg, beaten

For the filling and topping
500g cream cheese (e.g. Philadelphia)
500g mascarpone
200g golden caster sugar
2 large free-range eggs
2 tsps vanilla extract
zest and juice of 1 large lemon
400g raspberries, strawberries, tayberries
50g golden caster sugar

For the crust base, briefly process the first four ingredients
in a food processor, then add the egg and process again.
Remove from the processor and press into a buttered
24cm springform cake tin. Flouring your fingers, gently
ease the mixture a little way up the sides and covering all
the base. Prick lightly, then bake in a preheated oven
(180°C/350°F/Gas 4) for 15 minutes and remove. Don't

worry if the sides have collapsed a bit. Cool.

For the filling, beat everything (except the berries and 50g of the sugar) together with an electric mixer until smooth, then pour into the cooled tin. Bake at 150°C/300°F/Gas 2 for 1 hour, until, when shaken, the centre is still slightly wobbly. Switch off the oven, leave the cheesecake inside for about 2 hours, then remove and cool completely.

For the topping, place the berries and the remaining 50g of sugar in a saucepan and cook over a low heat, shaking the pan often to prevent sticking. Once the sugar has dissolved, cook for 1 minute, remove and cool. Spoon the topping over the cheesecake just before serving.

Redcurrant

Redcurrants are less common than they were in most gardens but are still grown in some traditional ones, and they are always found on fruit farms. Because of their strong, tart flavour, they are ideal in either savoury or sweet dishes. If they are to be frozen, use in a recipe that requires them to be sieved after cooking, as the stalks are difficult to remove after defrosting.

Redcurrant parfait

Serve with fresh berries and shortbread or tayberry coulis.

Serves 6–8
1.25kg redcurrants (on their stalks)
3 large free-range egg-yolks
150g icing sugar
450ml double cream, lightly whipped

First put the currants (still on their stalks – discard any stray leaves) in a large pan with about 100ml water and bring slowly to the boil. Simmer gently for 4–5 minutes, stirring, until the currants are soft.

Drain in a colander over a large bowl, retaining the liquid. Now puree the currants in a food processor (stalks and all; you are about to sieve them out) then place this puree into a large sieve over a bowl. Add 200ml of the retained liquid and push as much of the puree through as possible. Set this aside until required.

In a food mixer, whisk the yolks and sugar until pale and frothy, then add the redcurrant puree and combine well. Now fold in the cream, very gently but thoroughly; until blended.

Turn the mixture into two long loaf tins lined with clingfilm. Freeze until required. To serve, remove from the freezer about 20 minutes before serving, dip the outside in hot water and serve in slices.

Squishy meringue berry roll

Serve with extra berries and a jug of pouring cream.

Serves 6–8
6 medium free-range egg-whites
250g caster sugar
1 level tbsp cornflour
2 tsps lemon juice
100g chopped roasted hazelnuts

For the filling
300ml double cream, lightly whipped
100g mascarpone, beaten until smooth
25g caster sugar
350g strawberries (cut) and redcurrants, some currants still on sprigs

First prepare the baking sheet: line a Swiss roll tin (23 x 33cm) with baking parchment and lightly butter. Preheat the oven to 170°C/325°F/Gas 3.

Whisk the egg whites until you have soft peaks, then, whisking constantly, gradually add the sugar and whisk until it is thick and glossy. Fold in the cornflour and lemon juice. Spread this into the prepared tin, levelling the surface. Bake for 15 minutes until a pale golden brown.

Remove and cool for 5 minutes in the tin. Take a large piece of baking parchment and place it on your work surface. Sprinkle over the nuts (so that they are

roughly in the rectangular shape of the meringue). Turn
the meringue onto the nuts, carefully peel away the
parchment and leave to cool.

Mix the cream, mascarpone and sugar together and
spread over the cooled meringue. Scatter the berries and
stripped currants all over the top, then carefully roll up,
using the paper to help. Leave the paper on until the roll
has been well chilled. Chill for at least 6 hours, then
carefully remove the paper and slip onto a serving dish.
Decorate with sprigs of redcurrants and serve in slices
with extra fruit and cream.

Redcurrant apple lattice pie

For a perfect lattice, cut 10 strips of pastry, then, starting
at one side of the pie, place one in position. Set the next
strip over it at right angles, then return to the first side
and position the third strip. Continue by alternating the
side from which you start.

Serves 8
350g sweet shortcrust pastry
1 free-range egg-yolk
1 heaped tbsp semolina
750g cooking apples, peeled, cored and diced
500g redcurrants
150g caster sugar
milk and additional caster sugar

Roll out three-quarters of the pastry to fit a deep 24cm
loose-based cake tin. Prick all over and brush with the
egg-yolk all over the base and sides. Chill for an hour.
Roll out the remaining pastry and cut into 10 strips.
Place these on a floured board and chill with the pie for
an hour. Then remove from the fridge and sprinkle the
base with the semolina.

For the filling, mix the apples, redcurrants and sugar
and pile into the pie. Squish down if necessary, then place
the strips of pastry over the top to form the lattice. Brush
the top with milk and sprinkle over some caster sugar.

Bake at 180°C/350°F/Gas 4 for 50–60 minutes until

the pastry is golden brown. Cool for half an hour or so before decanting.

Serve with lightly whipped cream.

Strawberry

Although strawberries have always played second fiddle to the raspberry in Scotland, they are now much loved, and since they ripen earlier than the raspberry, are an ideal way to kick off the berry season in earnest! Only very few savoury dishes can take their natural sweetness, so use primarily in sweet dishes. They do not freeze well.

Strawberry daiquiri

Serves 3–4
100ml white rum
2 tbsps freshly squeezed lime juice
10 large strawberries
8 ice cubes, crushed
caster sugar, to taste

Place everything in a blender and hold the lid on tightly.
Process until smooth, then add enough sugar to sweeten
– I like one heaped teaspoon. Pour into chilled cocktail
glasses.

Strawberry risotto

This traditional dish is made using wild strawberries, but regular ones are fine.

Serves 2–3

2 tbsps olive oil
½ red onion, peeled and chopped
200g strawberries, hulled and quartered
150g carnaroli rice (or Arborio)
½ large glass red wine (about 100ml)
approx. 600ml light chicken (or vegetable) stock, hot
50g grated parmesan cheese

Place the oil in a pan and gently sauté the onions till soft. Add half the strawberries, stir, then add the rice and stir to coat in the fat.

Add the wine, stir over medium heat until it is evaporated, then reduce the heat to medium-low and start adding the hot stock a ladle at a time. Add just enough stock so that the rice is al dente and the risotto creamy. Stir often, adding some salt after 10 minutes or so.

Once the risotto is ready, remove from the heat and add the cheese and remaining strawberries. Now cover and leave for a couple of minutes.

Add plenty of freshly milled pepper and more salt if necessary and serve in warm bowls.

Berries with rosewater cream

Rosewater is now widely available in supermarkets and delis; dried rose petals can be got from herbalists or specialist Middle Eastern suppliers.

Serves 4–6
1kg mixed berries (strawberries, rasps, blueberries – and brambles
    later on in the season)
250g mascarpone, softened
rosewater, to taste
dried rose petals to garnish, optional

Pile the berries onto a shallow dish, stacking up as high as possible.

    Beat the mascarpone with enough rosewater to your preferred taste (1–2 tbsps), then place in a serving bowl. Garnish with a few dried rose petals if desired.

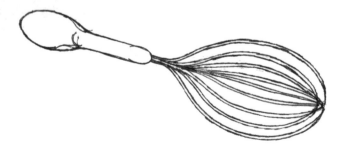

DRIED ROSE PETALS

Rose Water

Mascarpone

Chilled strawberry and mint soup

Perfect starter for lunch on a warm summer's day.

Serves 4
250g strawberries
a good handful of mint leaves
300ml natural yoghurt
300ml clear chicken stock, fat removed
½ tsp ground ginger
mint sprigs, to garnish

Puree the berries with the mint, then add the yoghurt and blend again.

Add the ginger to the stock in a pan and heat slowly until the ginger is dissolved. Cool, then add to the strawberry mixture. Season to taste and chill.

Chill four soup bowls and ladle in the chilled soup. Garnish with a sprig of mint – and plop an ice cube into each one if you like.

Strawberry, cream cheese and balsamic ice-cream

The vinegar complements the strawberries wonderfully, but be sure to use a good quality balsamic.

Serves 4–6
750g strawberries, hulled and sliced
75g caster sugar
2 tbsps aged/thick balsamic vinegar
300g cream cheese
2 tbsps fromage frais
300ml double cream
1 tbsp icing sugar, sifted

Toss the strawberries, sugar and vinegar together and leave for an hour or so if possible, then puree or blend in a food processor. Press through a fine sieve to eliminate the pips.

Beat the cream cheese and fromage frais till soft and then fold this into the puree.

Whip the cream and icing sugar till it is floppy, then fold into the strawberry mixture and churn in an ice-cream machine OR freeze in an ice-cream container, beating every half hour until solid.

Serve with fresh berries.

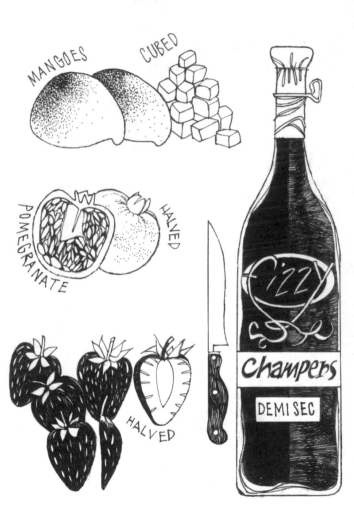

Strawberry, mango and champagne salad

Of course you can use any other fizz, such as Prosecco or cava.

Serves 4
450g strawberries, halved
2 large ripe mangoes, cubed
seeds and juice of half a pomegranate
glass of champagne (about 150ml)

Place the berries and mango in a pretty glass bowl, pour over the pomegranate juice and scatter with the seeds. Just before serving, pour over the wine and serve at once, while the bubbles are still hissing.

Strawberry and marshmallow salad

This is a fun salad that children and adults alike will adore!

Serves 4

350g strawberries, quartered
350g seedless grapes (halved if large)
50–75g mini marshmallows
3 tbsps freshly squeezed orange juice
edible flowers, optional

Place everything in a glass bowl, toss gently, then refrigerate before serving. Decorate with edible flowers if in season.

Berry tarts with bay cream

Use a selection of berries – I like halved strawberries, brambles and blueberries.

Serves 4
For the pastry
150g plain flour
75g icing sugar
50g ground almonds
125g butter, cubed

For the filling
2 free-range egg-yolks
50g caster sugar
25g plain flour
300ml milk
4 fresh bay leaves
2 tbsps mascarpone
350–400g mixed berries

For the pastry, place the first three ingredients in a food processor, blitz, then add butter and blitz again until it resembles breadcrumbs. Add enough very cold water (1–2 tbsps, roughly) to combine to a ball. Remove from the processor and chill, then roll out and use to line 4 x 10cm loose-base tart tins. Prick the pastry and chill again.

Line with foil and baking beans and bake at 190°C/375°F/Gas 5 for 15 minutes, remove the foil and beans and continue to bake for a further 5–10 minutes until cooked through. Cool and remove from the tins.

For the filling, mix the yolks, sugar and flour together. In a heavy saucepan, heat the milk and bay leaves slowly, and once you see bubbles, remove from the heat. Very slowly add the egg mixture, whisking constantly. Cook over a low heat for 4–5 minutes, whisking all the time, till thickened and lump-free. Remove the bay leaves and tip the mixture into a bowl, covering closely with clingfilm.

Just before serving, mix the custard with the mascarpone and divide between the tartlets. Top with berries and serve.

Red fruit salad

You can add raspberries or tayberries to this mix.

Serves 4
500g strawberries, hulled and sliced
450g red plums and black grapes, sliced
1 tbsp caster sugar
2 tbsps orange juice

Place the fruit in a bowl, spoon over the sugar and
orange juice, toss well and leave for about half an hour or
so. Serve at room temperature with thick yoghurt.

Strawberries with lavender ice-cream

You can garnish with extra lavender flowers if you like.

Serves 4
600ml double cream
10g lavender flowers
4 tbsps runny honey
350g strawberries, sliced

Bring 300ml of the cream slowly to the boil. When you start to see bubbles, remove from the heat. Place the lavender flowers in a wide jug and pour the cream over them. Allow to cool, stirring often.

Once cold, strain into a bowl and refrigerate until very cold. Add the remaining cream to the lavender cream and whip together until it forms soft peaks. Then gently fold in the honey. Pour into a shallow freezer container, seal and freeze for 4–5 hours, without stirring, until firm. Soften slightly in the fridge, before serving with a topping of strawberries.

Whole strawberry jam

Strawberry jam is probably everyone's favourite jam, but many people are extremely wary about making it, for fear of having jars of runny jam. But ever since jam sugar (with added pectin) was invented, the life of the jam maker has been made easier. For instead of adding liquid pectin or lemon juice to compensate for the low pectin in strawberries, you need simply to use the same method as you do in most jams – i.e. equal quantities of fruit to sugar. The other handy thing about the jam sugar is that, unlike raspberry jam (the other favourite – well, it is in my family), which you have to boil for up to 20 minutes before setting-point is reached, with strawberry jam it is boiled for a mere 4 minutes.

Scooping out whole strawberries is one of the perks of opening a fresh pot of jam.

To sterilise jam jars, I put them through a full cycle in the dishwasher, and dry thoroughly. I then warm them in the microwave just before potting. Alternatively, they can be washed and then thoroughly dried in a low oven for 30 minutes.

Makes 5 x 350g/12oz jars
1kg fresh strawberries, hulled
1kg jam sugar (i.e. with added pectin)
knob of butter

Place the strawberries in a large saucepan or preserving pan in layers with the sugar and leave for an hour or so, stirring once.

Place the pan over a low heat and, stirring often, heat gently until the sugar dissolves. During this time, mash down about half the berries, leaving the rest whole.

Once the sugar is all dissolved, increase the heat to maximum, add the butter (which disperses the scum) and bring to a full rolling boil (i.e. when the mixture rises and cannot be stirred down). Boil like this for 4 minutes, stirring occasionally, until setting-point.

After 4 minutes, remove the pan from the heat and test for setting: place a good dribble of jam on a cold saucer, leave for a minute or two, then push a finger through it. If the surface wrinkles and a clear line is left through the jam, it is ready. (If not, reboil for another minute, then test again.)

Leave the jam to stand for about 25 minutes, then stir and pot in warmed, sterilised jars. Wipe clean with a damp cloth.

Once completely cold, cover tightly and label. Store somewhere cool and dark.

Tayberry

A relatively recent berry, developed in the 1960s and 70s at Invergowrie on the River Tay, they are a cross between a bramble (blackberry) and a raspberry, not dissimilar to the loganberry. They freeze well.

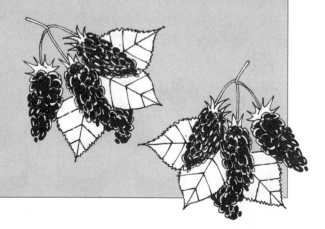

Tayberry coulis

Serve this with Redcurrant Parfait or with any berry ice-creams.

Serves 4–6
350g tayberries (or half raspberries and half brambles)
75g icing sugar, sifted
juice of half a lemon
good sploosh of gin

Place everything except the gin into a liquidiser or food processor and blend until smooth. Push through a sieve, then add gin and more sugar if required. Chill well before serving.

Blackberry + Raspberry = Tayberry

Warm berry compote
with rose-petal ice-cream

This ice-cream tastes exotic and perfumed, yet is
seriously easy to make. All you need are a couple of
scented roses (damask or other old-fashioned varieties are
best), some cream, sugar and a dash of rosewater.
Remember that most hothouse roses will have been
sprayed, so avoid these at all costs. Pick garden roses soon
after they have flowered and long before the petals fall
off. Although all rose petals are edible, you should be
guided by your nose: if the petals have a strong perfume,
they will add plenty of alluring fragrance to your recipe.
Choose either red or deep pink for the best visual effect.

Serves 4
For the ice-cream
2 scented, unsprayed roses
425ml double cream
100g icing sugar, sifted
2 tbsps natural yoghurt
rosewater (available from chemists)

For the compote
125g tayberries
125g black/redcurrants
125g blueberries
100ml gin
50g caster sugar
125g strawberries

For the ice-cream, remove the petals from the roses: very gently wash and rinse them if necessary. Trim off the white part at the base of each petal. Place the petals in a heavy saucepan with the cream and bring slowly to the boil. When you see bubbles, remove from the heat. Pour the contents into a bowl. When cold, place in the refrigerator for at least two hours, preferably overnight. Strain the cream, reserving the petals.

Whip the cream with the icing sugar until it forms soft peaks. Stir in the yoghurt, then add rosewater to taste: 2-3 teaspoons should be enough, depending on its strength. Gently fold in the petals. Pour into a freezer container, seal and freeze for at least five hours or until solid – you don't even have to stir it. Serve with the warm compote.

For the compote, place the first five ingredients in a saucepan. Slowly heat until the sugar dissolves, then increase the heat and bubble for 1 minute. Remove from the heat and stir in the strawberries.

Tayberry and blackcurrant slump

This is a wonderful pudding that can be made either
with fresh fruit in summer or with thawed frozen fruit in
winter. It can also be made with brambles or loganberries
instead of tayberries – and blueberries instead of blackcurrants.

When it emerges from the oven, the fruit is bubbling
in a puddle of crimson juices and the mascarpone is
oozing seductively out from a light cobbler-like scone
topping. Because the mascarpone is there, nestled
between fruit and scone, you do not need any cream
with this. It is a gloriously self-contained pudding.

And before you ask – a slump does just that.

Serves 6
450g tayberries
250g blackcurrants
50g golden caster sugar

For the topping
175g self-raising flour, sifted
1 level tsp baking powder
50g golden caster sugar
grated zest and juice of 1 lemon
50g butter, melted
1 large free-range egg, beaten
250g tub of mascarpone

Place the berries and currants in a pan with the sugar and very slowly heat until the sugar is dissolved and the juices run. Tip into an ovenproof dish and allow to cool.

Combine the flour, baking powder and sugar, then stir in the lemon zest. Add the melted butter, egg and lemon juice and combine gently.

Tip the mascarpone into a bowl and beat until smooth, then drop 6 tablespoonfuls over the fruit mixture; resist the urge to join them all together.

Cover each blob with a spoonful of the scone mixture: don't worry if it does not exactly cover the mascarpone, it will spread out a little as it cooks anyway.

Bake at 220°C/425°F/Gas 7 for about 20 minutes or until the fruit is bubbling and the mascarpone oozing out from the golden-brown crusted topping. Wait for 5 minutes, then serve.